Never Stop Dreaming

Jill Wilson

Special thanks to Telluride Arts for their generous contribution and continuing efforts to support local artists.

Illustrations copyright © 2021 Abby J. Fox. All rights reserved. No part of this book may be reproduced or used in any manner without written permission of the author or illustrator.

Printed in PRC via Print Ninja.

www.thetelluridealphabet.com

The Telluride Alphabet

An illustrated journey through Telluride's past and present

Written by Jill Wilson　　　Illustrated by Abby J. Fox

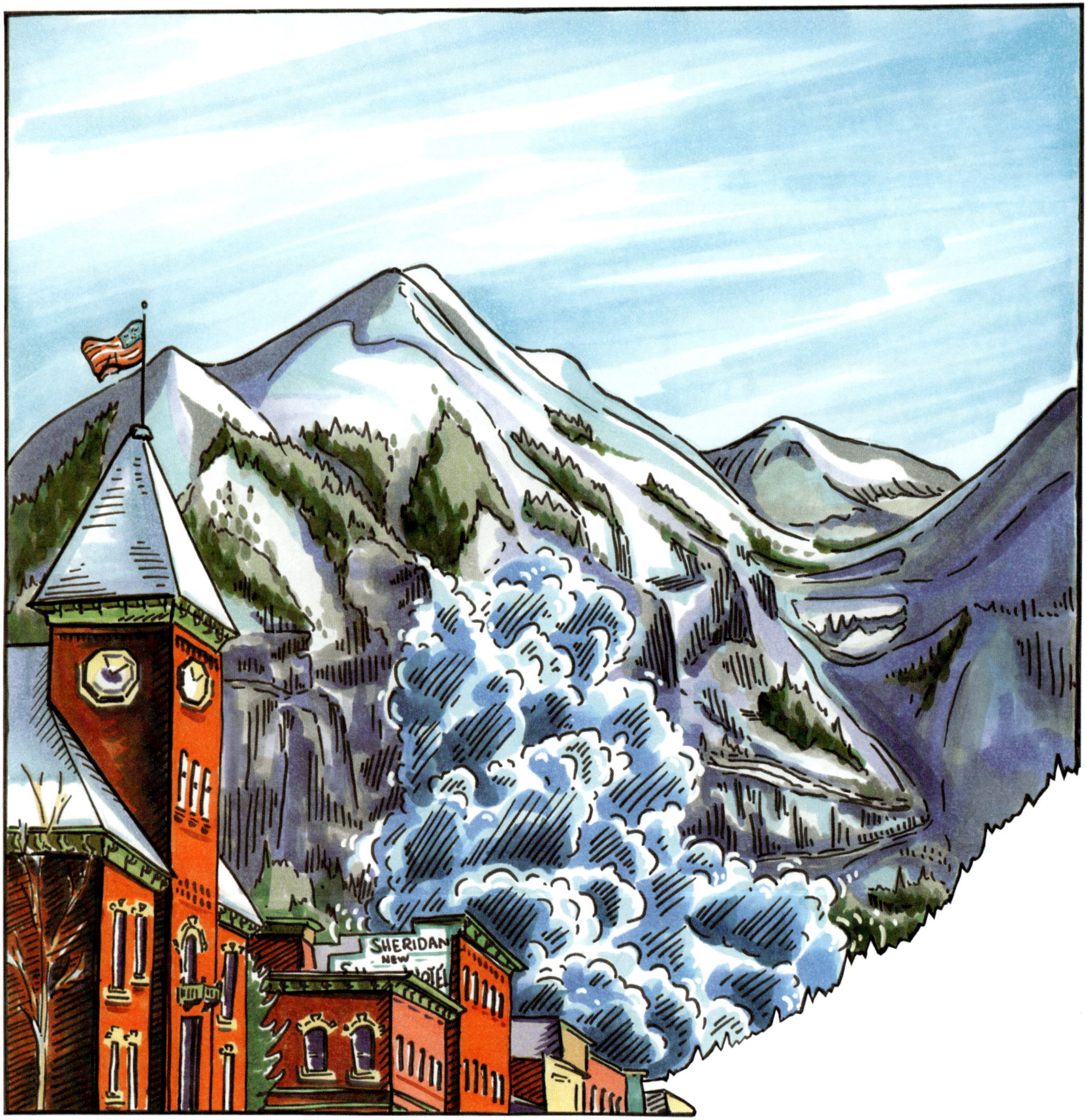
SHERIDAN
NEW

Astonishing Ajax

Ajax is the iconic peak that overlooks the Town of Telluride from 12,785 feet. Keep your eyes on it in the wintertime as you might spot an avalanche sliding down its steep cliff face in an explosive display of nature. In the summer, you can make the trek up to Ajax's summit if you're feeling adventurous. Be sure to catch the evening alpenglow, when the sunset casts a glorious pink hue upon the peak. It really is picture perfect.

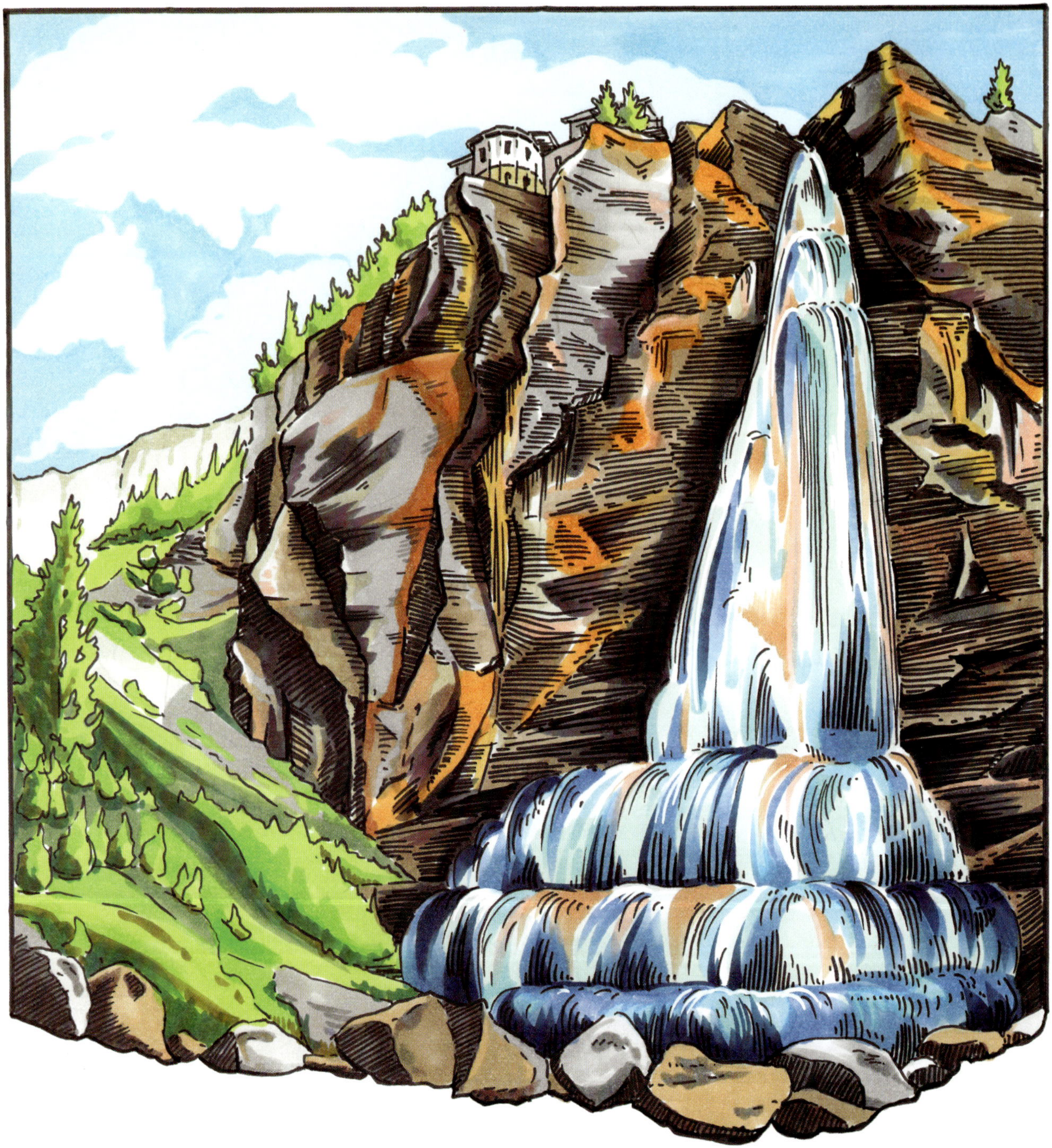

Booming Bridal Veil

At 365 feet, the stunning Bridal Veil Falls is officially the tallest freefalling waterfall in Colorado. The Smuggler-Union hydroelectric power plant perched atop the falls was built in 1907, making it one of the oldest alternating current facilities in the country. The first hydroelectric plant to produce and transmit AC power began operating in 1891 in Ames, just outside of Telluride. To get to the falls, hike or drive to the East End of town to get a close up look and feel the mist on your face.

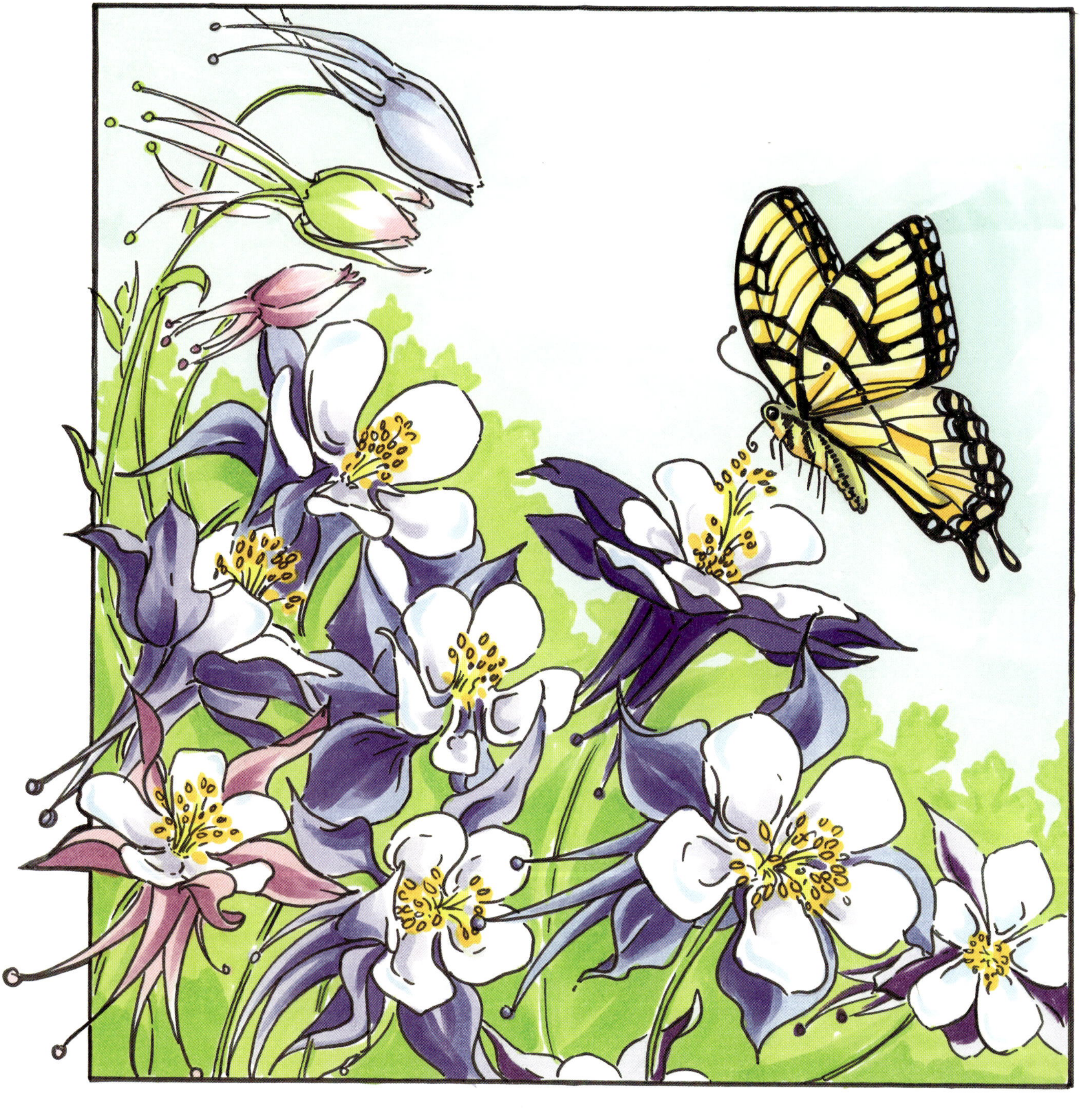

Captivating Columbines

Deriving from the Latin word "columba," meaning dove, the columbine was designated Colorado's state flower in 1899 by a group of school children. The blossom's unique shape is enticing for pollinators such as butterflies, hummingbirds and bees. Columbines come in a variety of vivid colors including blue, yellow, pink and purple. See how many different shades of columbines you can spot when you are hiking around Telluride in the late spring and early summer.

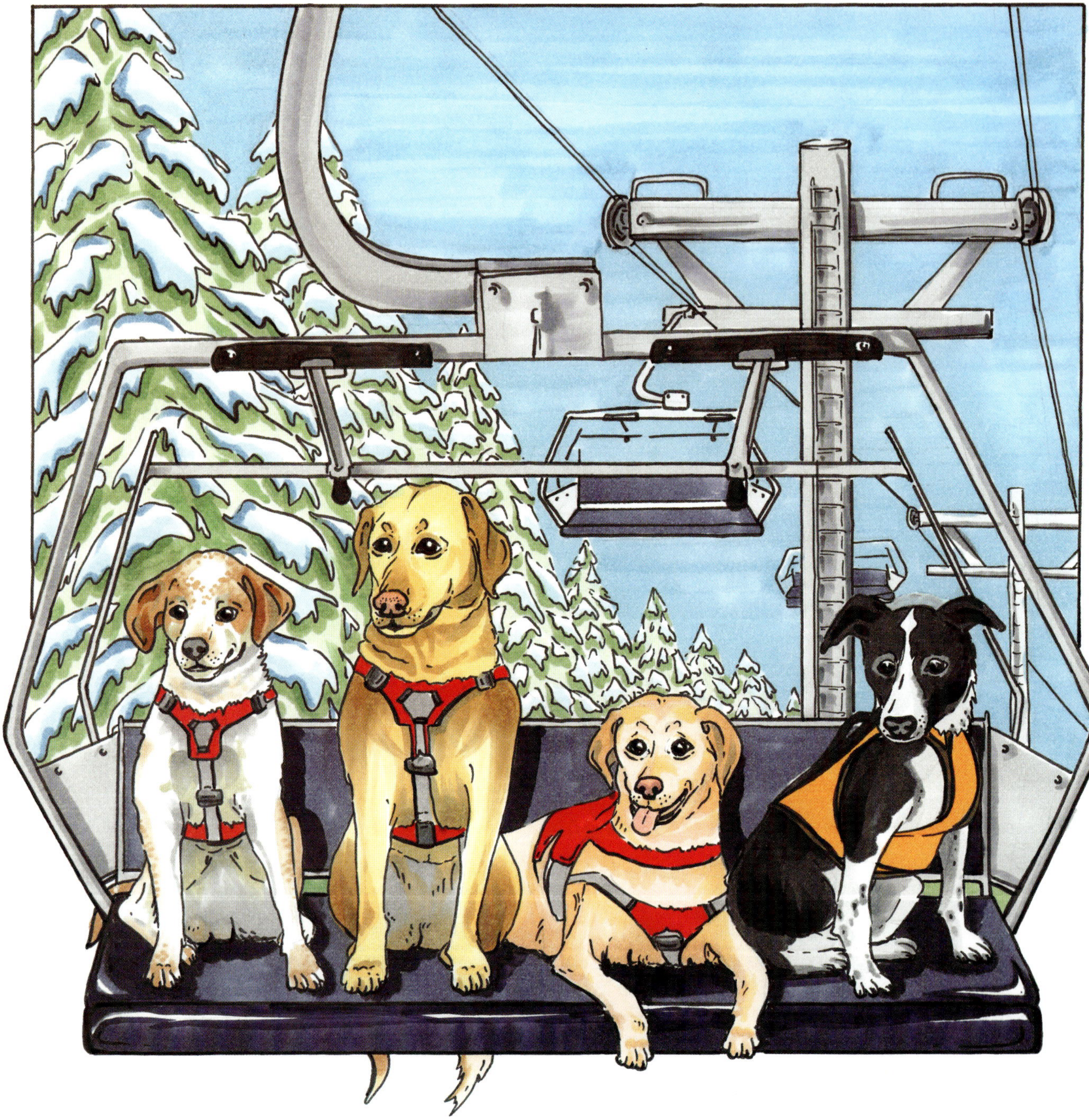

Daring Dogs

Lady Jane

The Telluride Avalanche Dogs are trained to perform under pressure to locate buried avalanche victims using their acute sense of smell. Labradors, golden retrievers, shepherds and collies tend to be the dogs of choice for mountain rescue teams due to their natural instincts to seek out and find. An avalanche dog can typically search around 2.5 acres in 30 minutes, about the size of two football fields. They are so well trained, they can even ride on helicopters, snowmobiles and chairlifts.

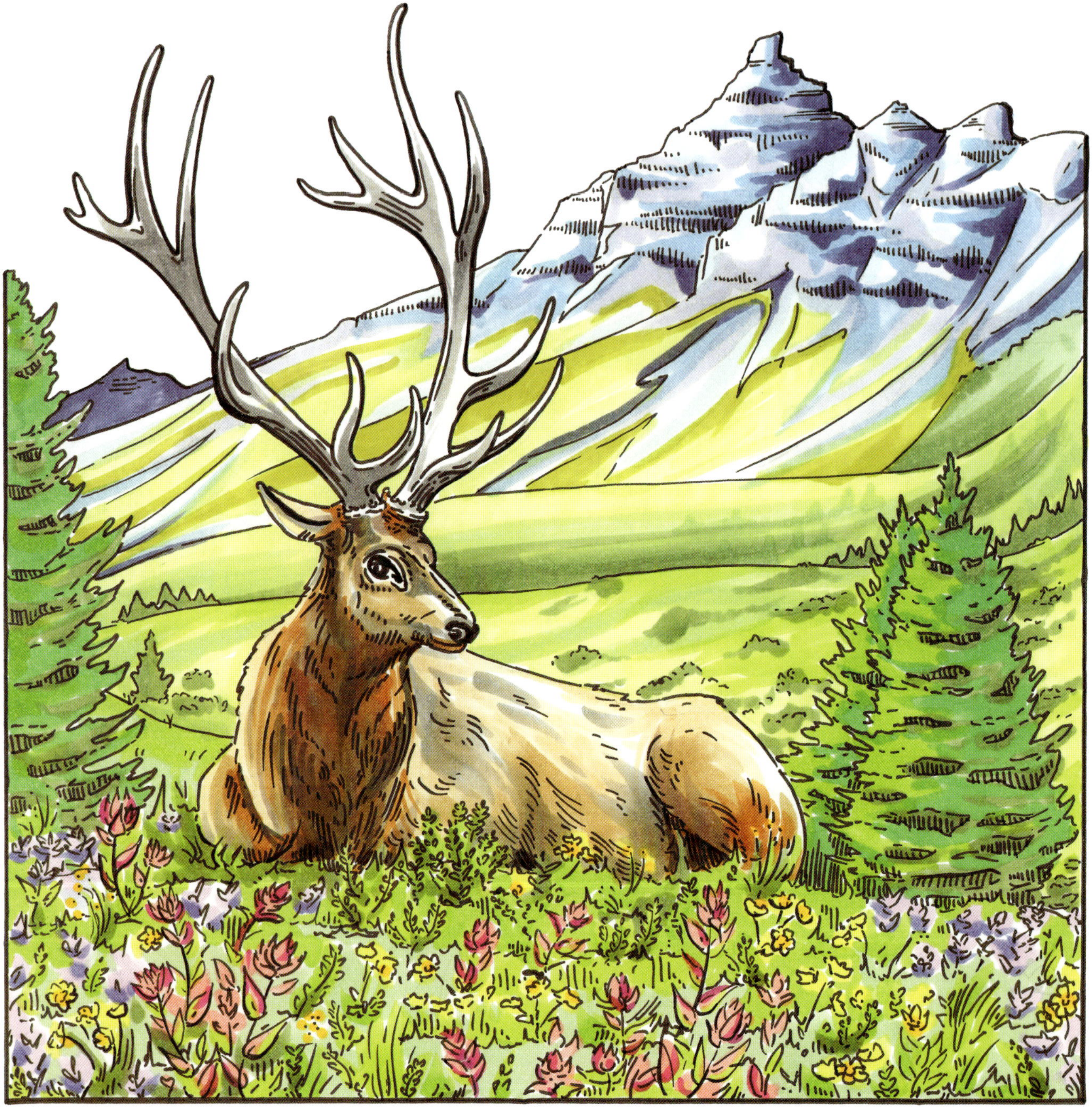

Elegant Elk

Elk are large mammals in the deer family that live in and around the forests of Colorado. They are also known as wapiti, meaning "white rump," a name given to them by the Shawnee. In the summer and fall, you can see large herds of elk roaming and lounging on the Valley Floor. If you listen closely, you may even hear the rutting call of the bulls, known as bugling. They are majestic creatures, but make sure to keep your distance because they are wild animals and their behavior can be unpredictable .

FREE BOX

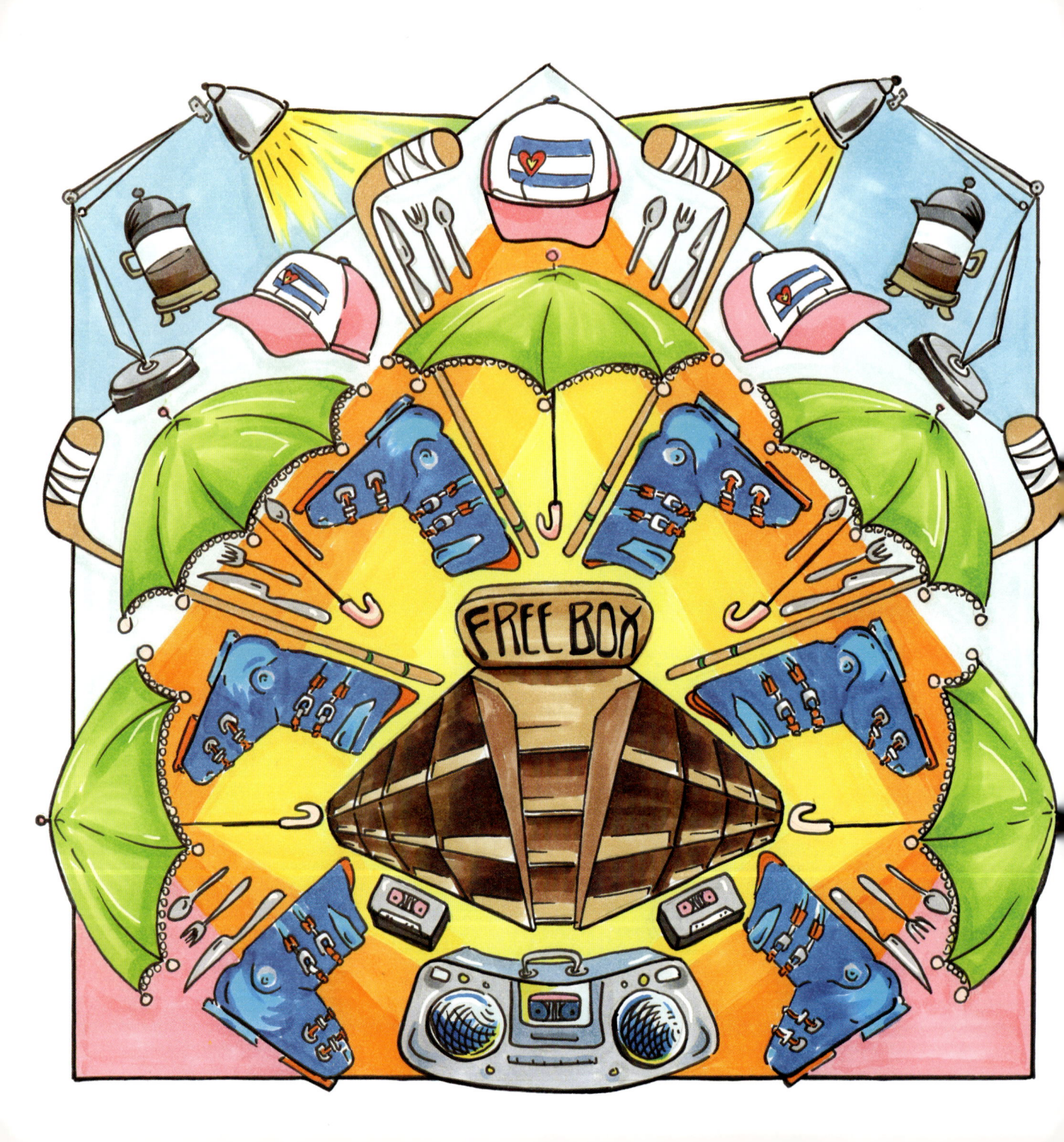

Funky Free Box

In the 1970s, the Free Box grew from a simple cardboard box to the cubby-like structure that we have known and loved for for years. Sitting at the corner of Pine Street and Colorado Avenue, the Free Box is a great way to reduce, reuse, and recycle. Locals say "the Free Box provides", as it seems to always have precisely what you need. It's especially bountiful in between seasons when people are leaving town or cleaning out their closets. What's the sweetest thing you've ever scored from the Free Box?

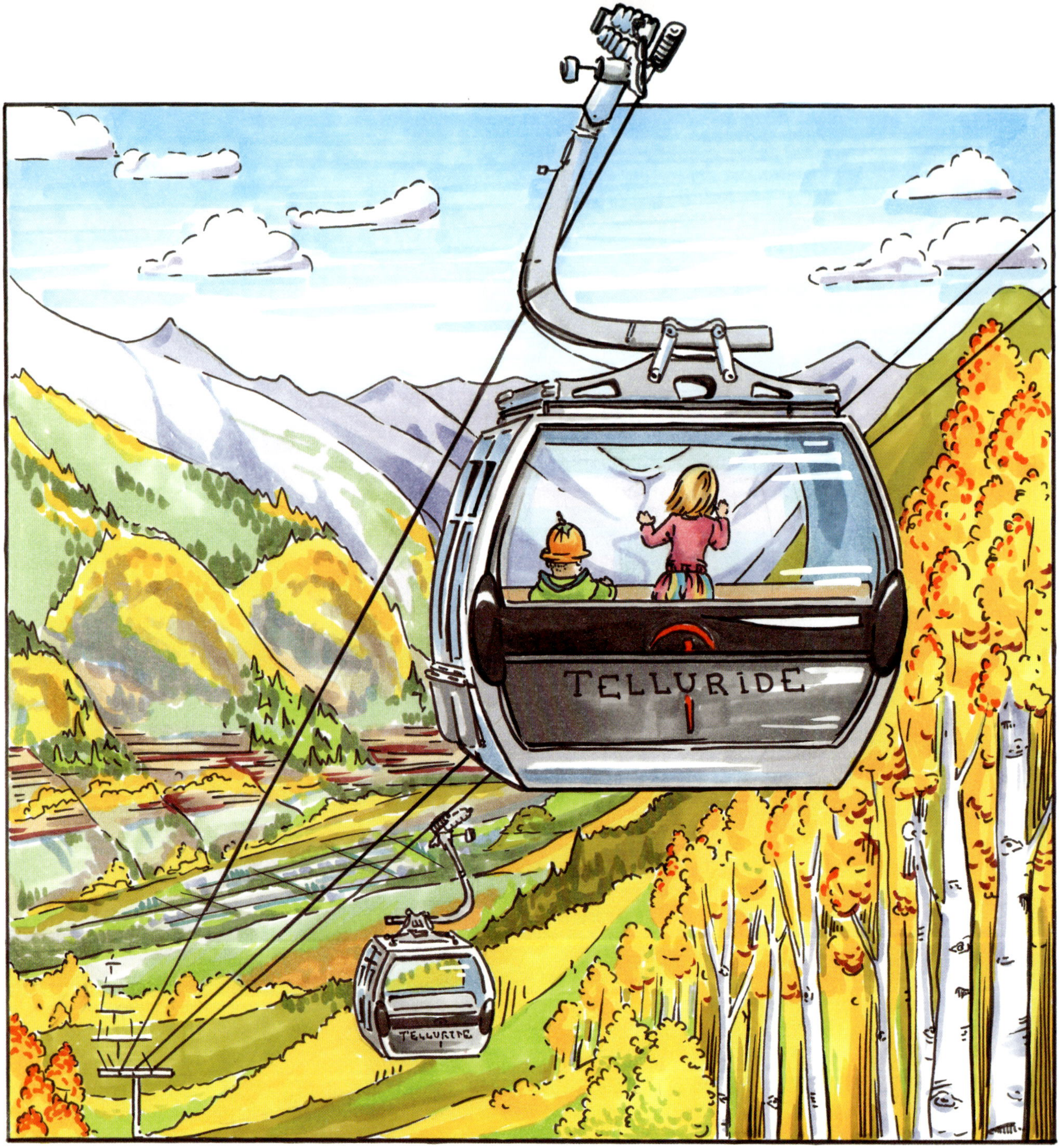
TELLURIDE

Gliding Gondola

The gondola has been praised for providing free, convenient and environmentally sound transportation since it opened in 1996. It links the historic Town of Telluride to the Town of Mountain Village in a 2.4 mile, 12 minute, awe-inspiring journey. From the gondola's highest point, San Sophia Station, you can hike, bike or ski down to either town, depending on the season. You can even bring your furry friends on the gondola, just make sure to grab a cabin marked with animal paws.

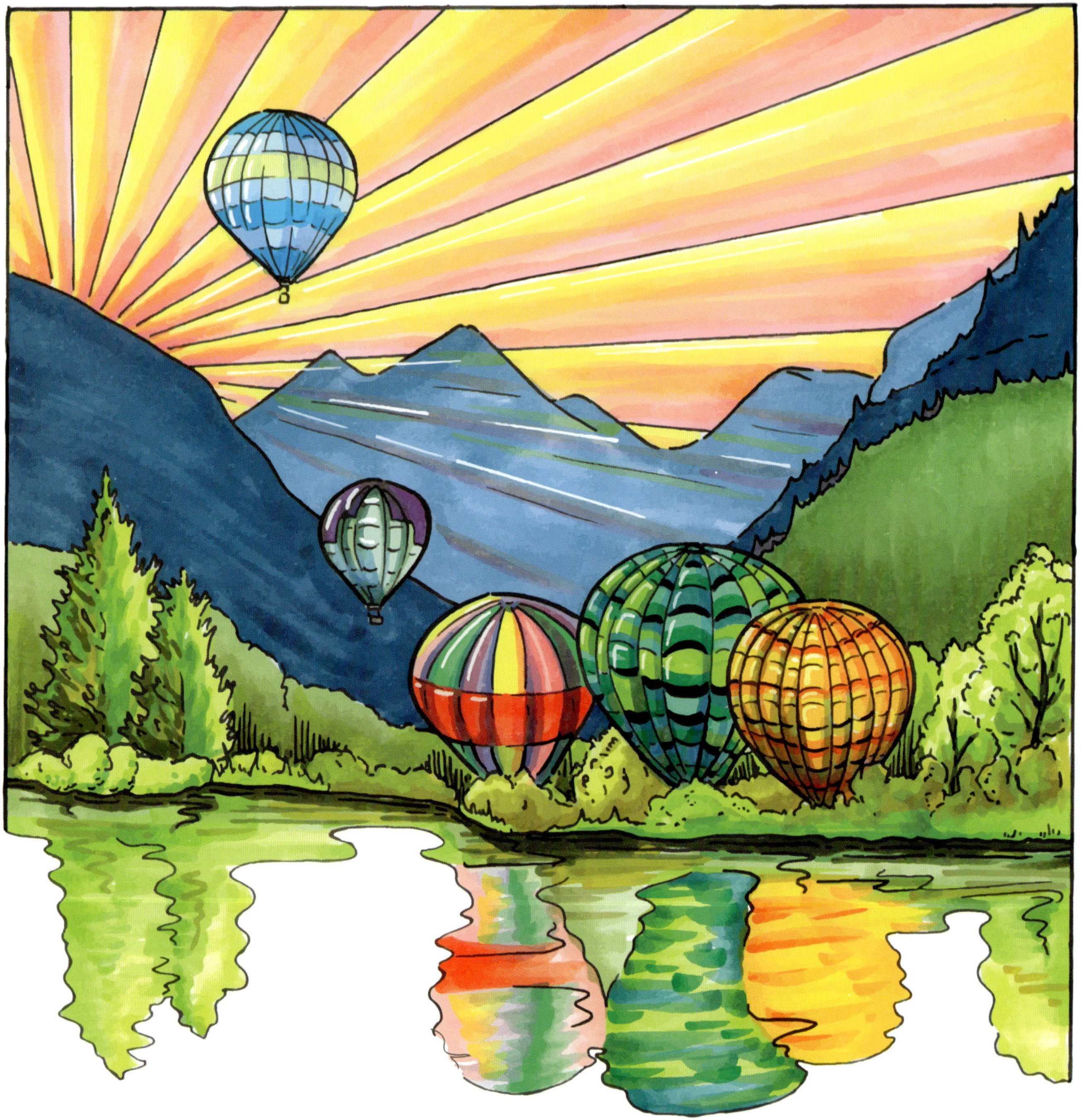

Hovering Hot Air Balloons

Look to the sky during Telluride's Hot Air Balloon Festival, held in early June. Weather permitting, dozens of hot air balloons launch from Town Park at sunrise and sail down the valley, landing about a mile west of town. If you're lucky, you might even be able to catch a ride in one of the balloons by getting up extra early to volunteer. You won't want to miss Saturday night of the festival, when the pilots inflate their balloons along Main Street and fire up the propane in a sensational event called "The Glow."

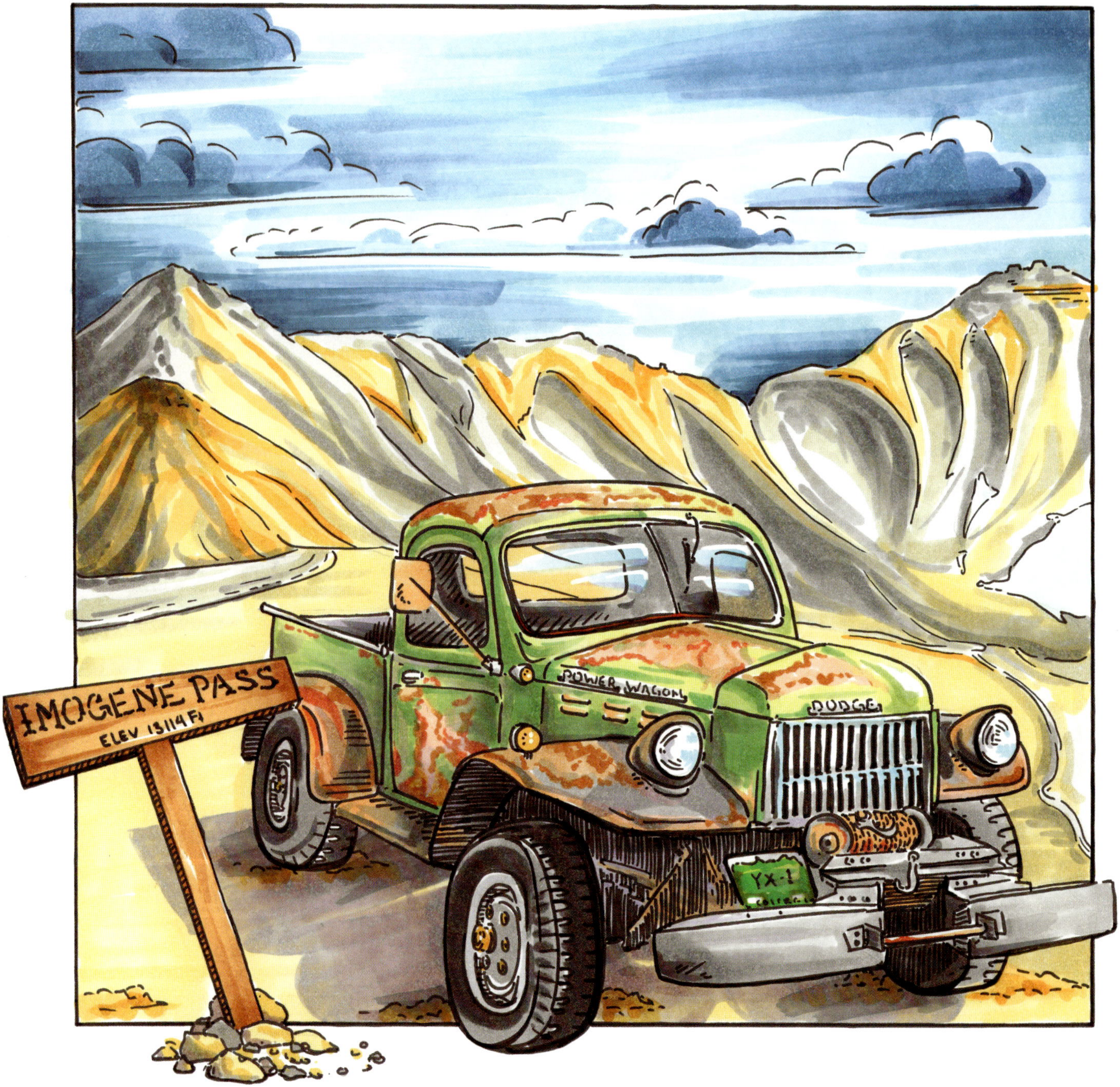
IMOGENE PASS
ELEV 13114 Ft
POWER WAGON
DODGE
YX-1

Impressive Imogene

Named after the wife of one of the partners in the Camp Bird Mine, Imogene Pass sits at an elevation of 13,114 feet. In 1880, Tomboy Road was constructed to connect the towns of Telluride and Ouray. You can drive your own high clearance vehicle over the pass, or you can take a guided tour if you want to sit back and enjoy the views. If you really want to get your blood pumping, sign up for the Imogene Pass Run. This 17.1 mile race challenges competitors to traverse the old mining road, racking up over a vertical mile of elevation gain along the way.

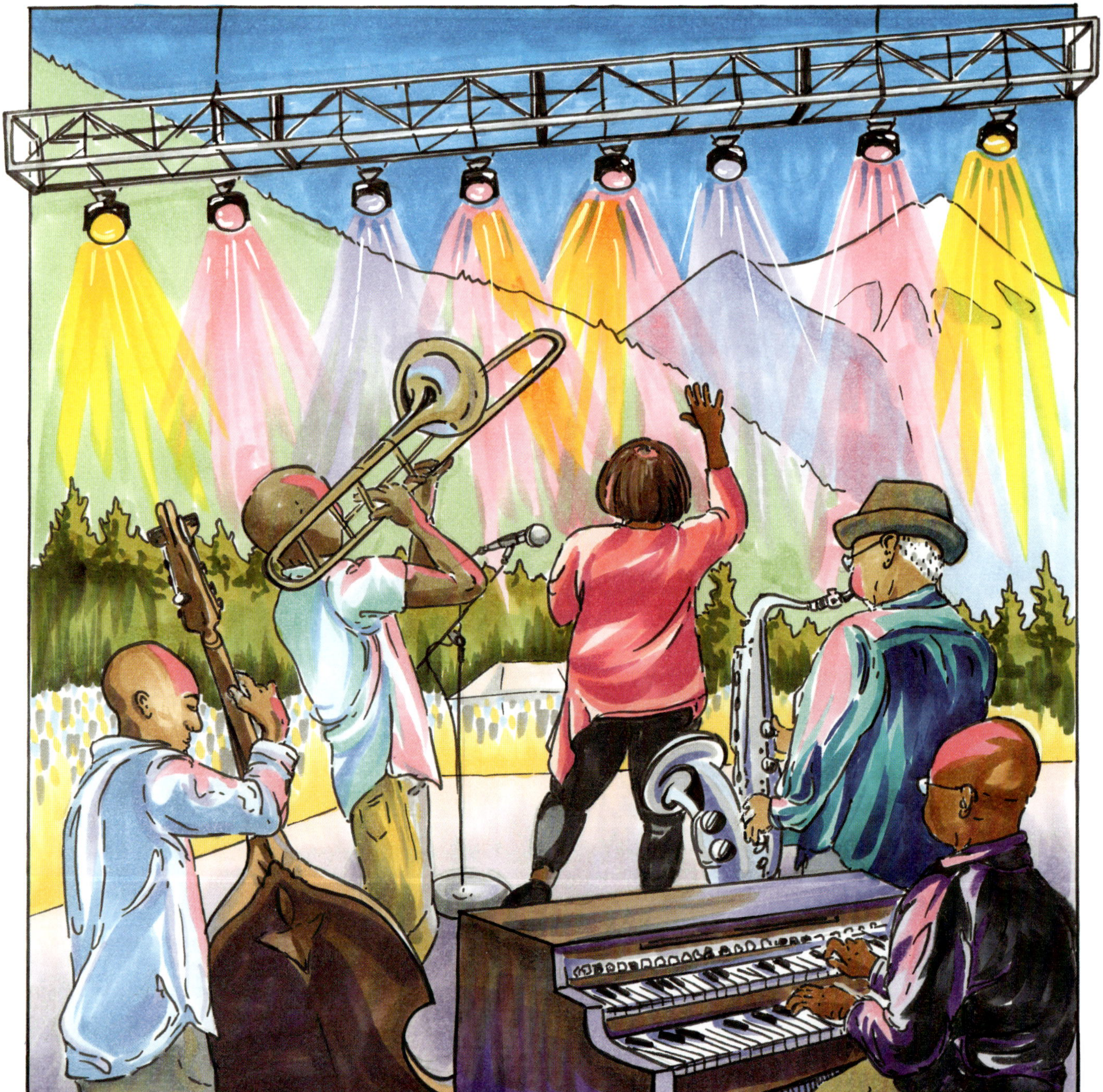

Joyous Jubilees

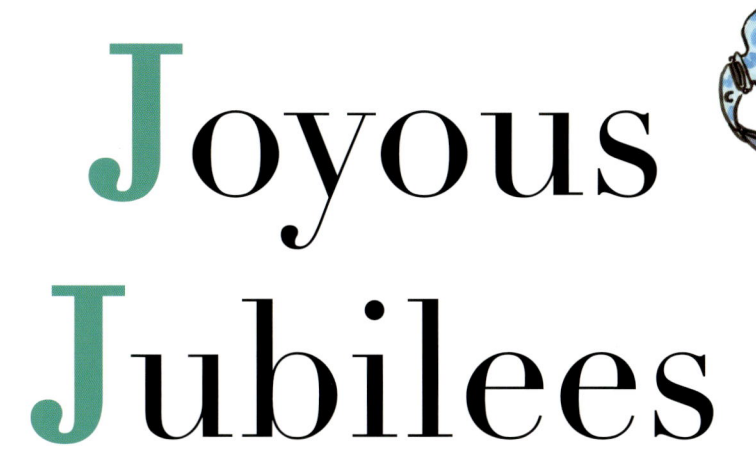

The historic Fred Shellman Memorial Stage in Town Park has been the picturesque setting for summer music festivals, such as the long-running Bluegrass Festival in June, RIDE Festival in July, Jazz Fest in August, and Blues and Brews in September. It doesn't get much better than jamming out to live music in a setting like Telluride, where the rich melodies and sunsets ricochet off the surrounding box canyon walls. Join the early morning tarp runners to secure your primo real estate at the festivals.

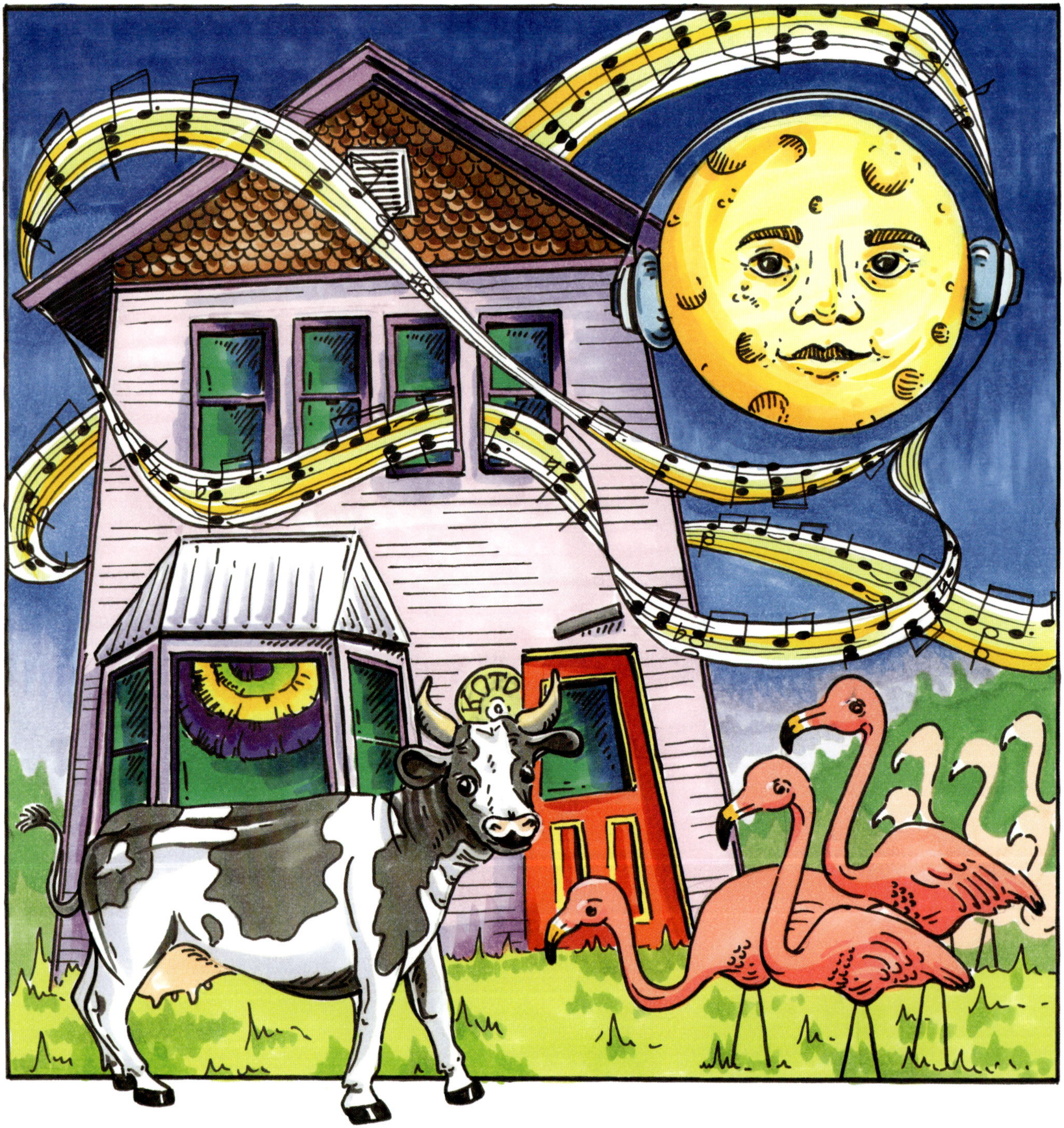
KOTO

Kooky KOTO

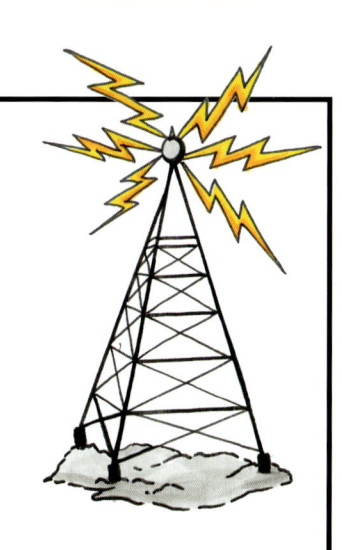

KOTO radio, located in the "Purple House on Pine," has provided the Telluride area with high quality, commercial-free broadcasting since 1975. Tune your dial to 91.7FM to listen to some funky beats spun by your favorite, local DJs. The station is staffed by a group of dedicated professionals, fueled by enthusiastic volunteers, and supported by listener donations. Celebrate the end of Telluride's ski season by busting a move at KOTO's flamingo themed street dance.

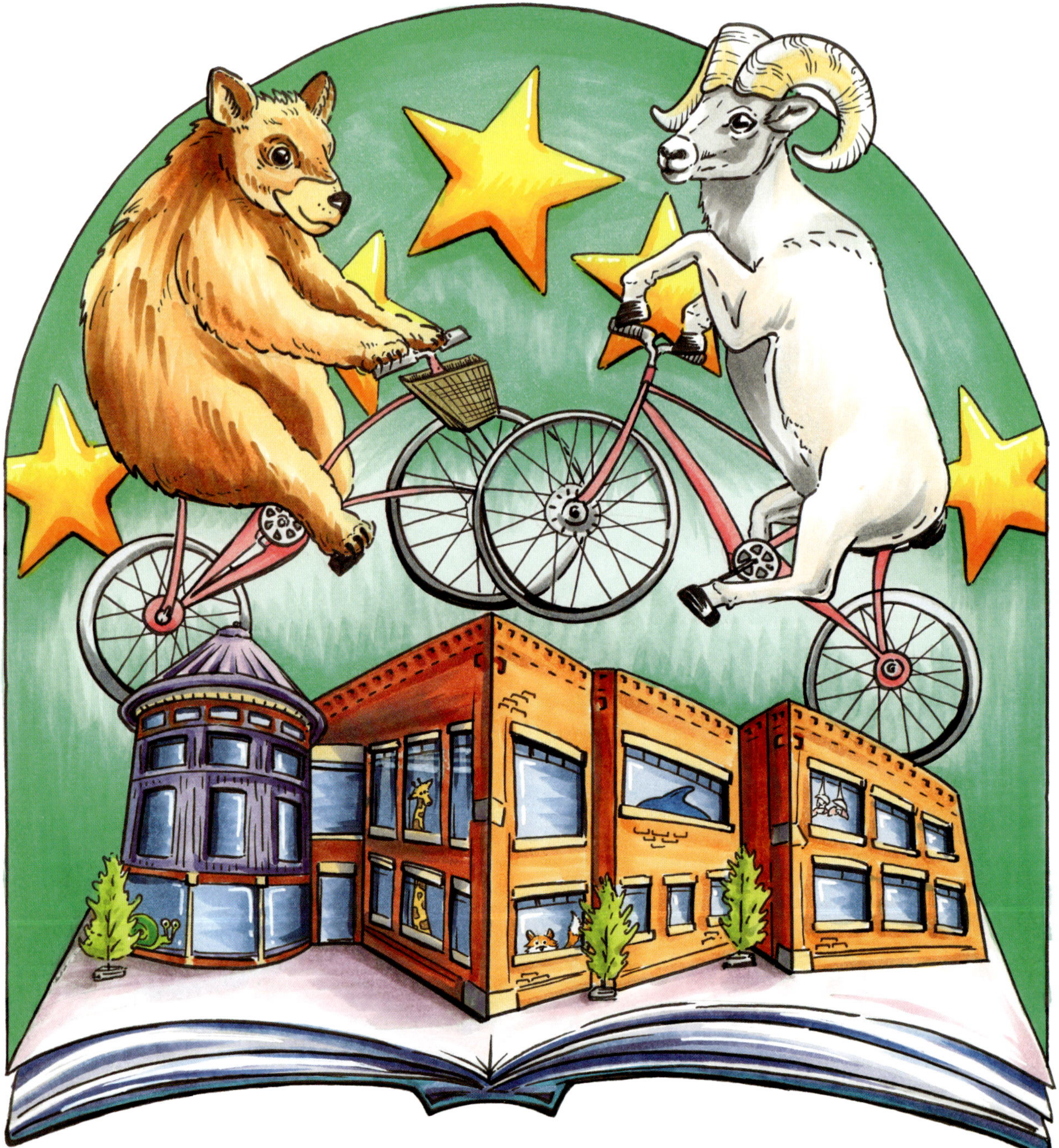

Legendary Library

Came to ski, stayed for the library

The Wilkinson Public Library is named to honor the founders, Larry and Betty Wilkinson, whose dream of starting a public library in Telluride came true in 1972. From its humble start in a Quonset hut, the library moved to the former town jail, and is now in the beloved brick building that acts as a community hub for both locals and visitors. This 5-Star Library truly has something for everyone. You can even check out unusual items such as snowshoes in the winter and bicycles in the summer.

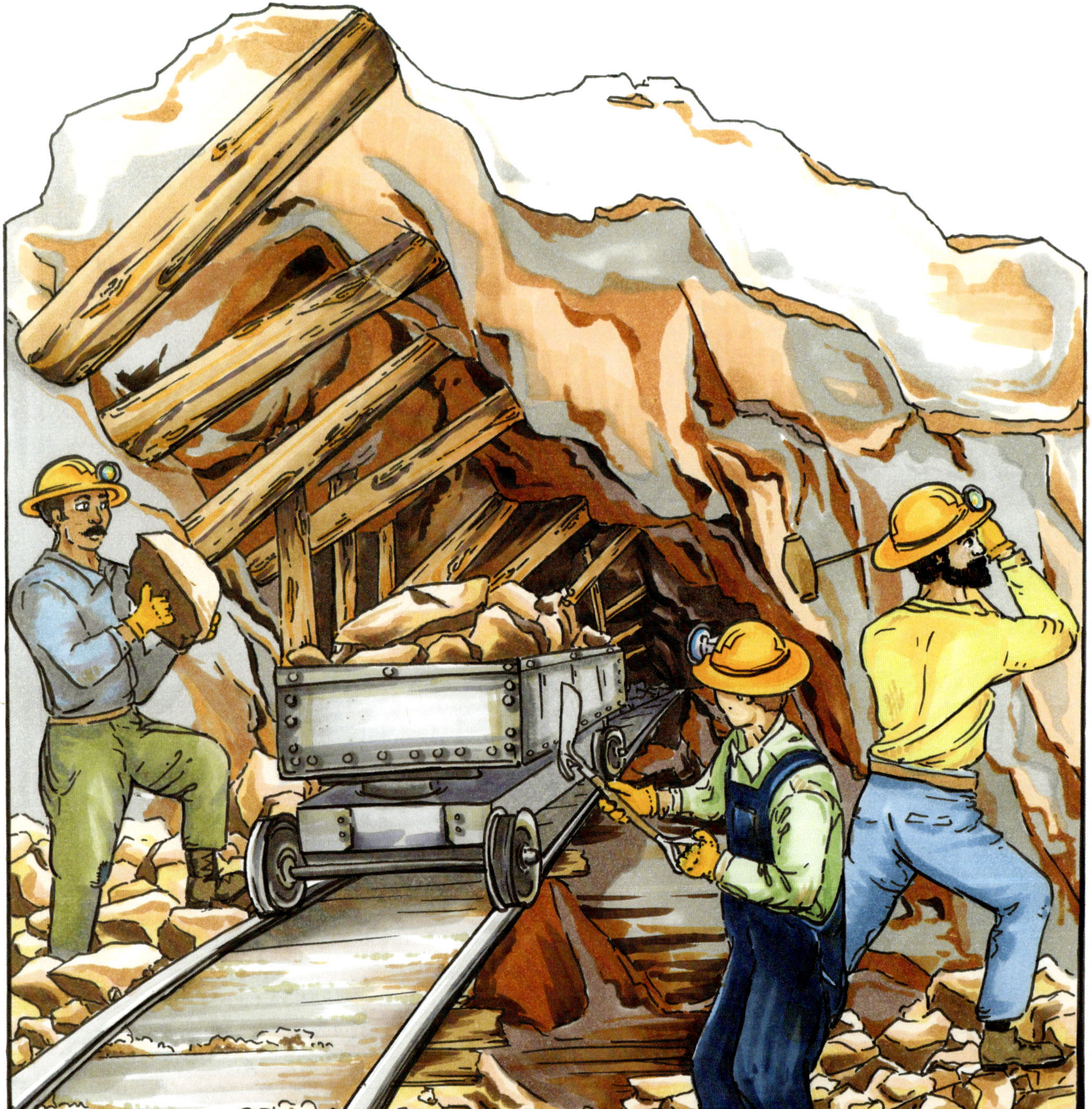

Mighty Miners

Prospector John Fallon made the first mining claim in the Marshall Basin above Telluride in 1875. The town of Columbia was established as a mining camp in 1878 and was later renamed Telluride in 1887, allegedly after the mineral Tellurium. The arrival of the railroad in 1890 greatly accelerated the mining industry in Telluride, and by the end of the 1890s there were 204 mines operating in the area. Although there are no longer any active mines, there are still over 350 miles of mining tunnels running beneath the mountains of Telluride to this day.

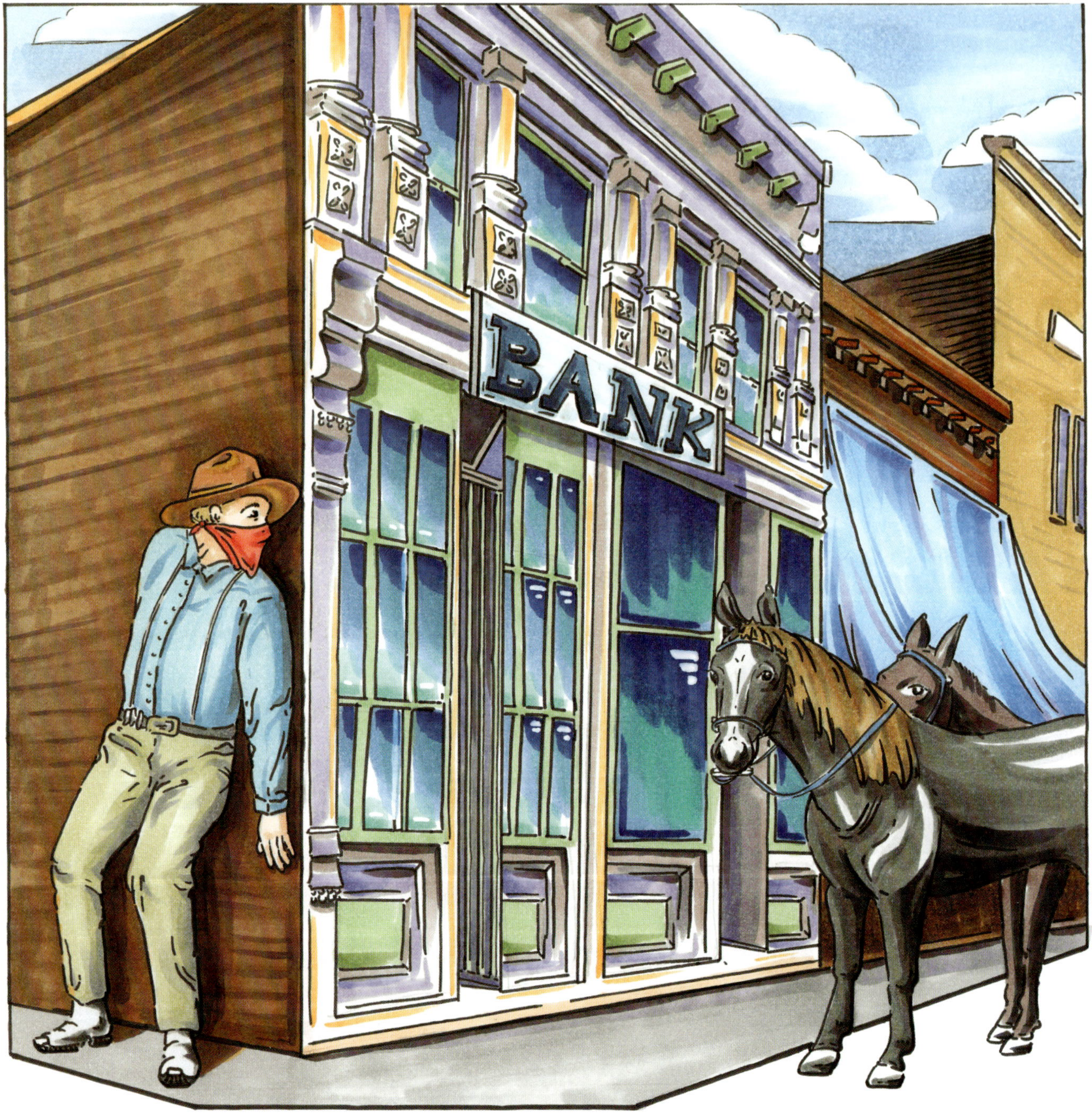
BANK

Notorious Nabbers

On June 24, 1889, Matt Warner, Tom McCarty, and Robert LeRoy Parker, better known as Butch Cassidy, robbed the San Miguel Valley Bank on the main street of Telluride. The "Wild Bunch" made out with close to $20,000, which translates to around half a million dollars today. Although the bank burned down shortly after the heist, it is commemorated with a plaque at its original location of 129/131 West Colorado Avenue. To learn more about Telluride's rowdy past, check out the Telluride Historical Museum at the top of North Fir Street.

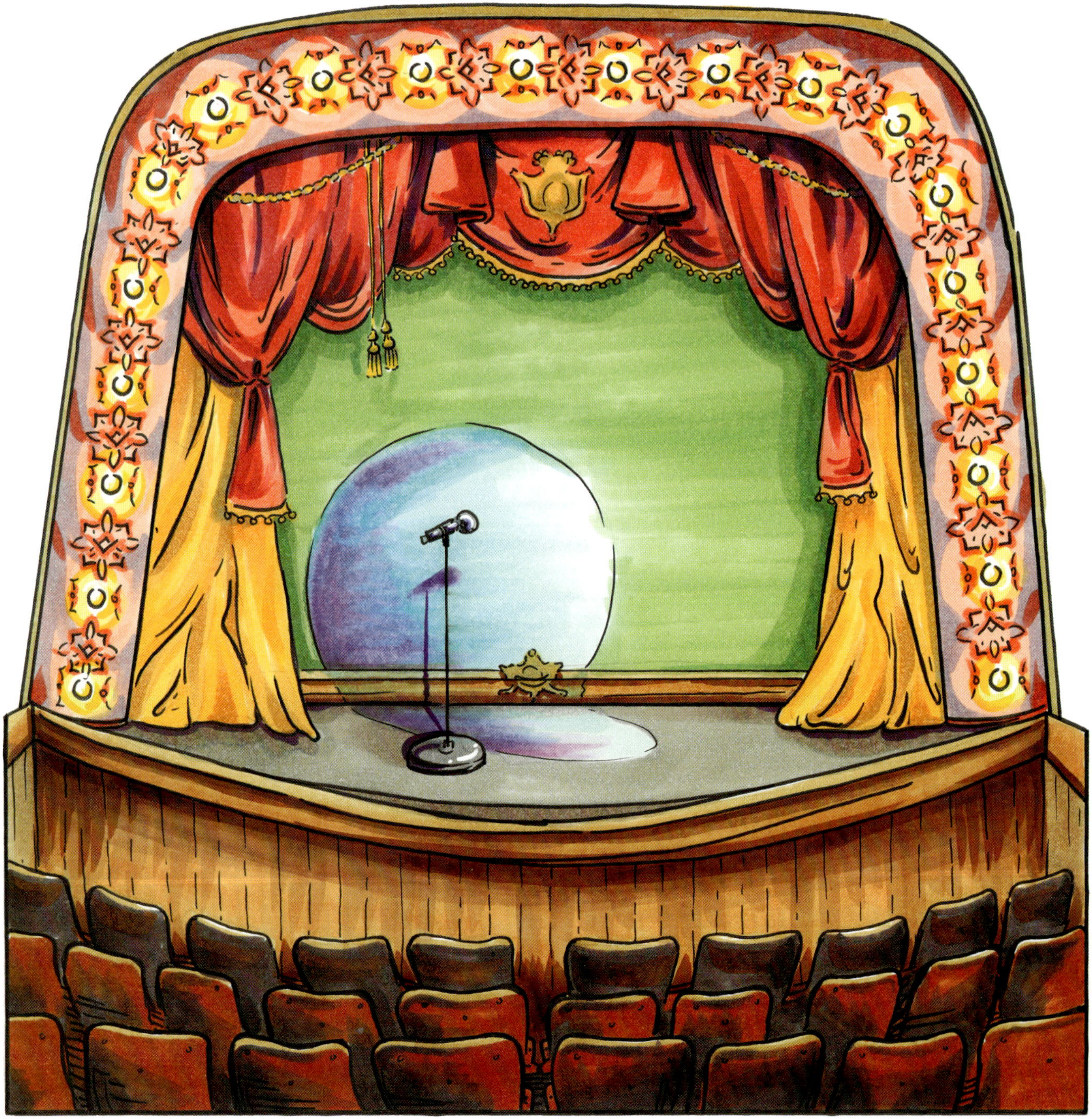

Opulent Opera House

Originally named the Segerberg Opera House, this lavish building was constructed in 1913 to provide entertainment for the townspeople of Telluride. Following a glamorous renovation, it was renamed the Sheridan Opera House after the neighboring hotel. Today, the Opera House is a popular venue for world renowned live music, vivacious local theater, exclusive movie premieres, and a menagerie of exuberant events. Although Telluride is a small town, the Opera House does an outstanding job of bringing in big city culture.

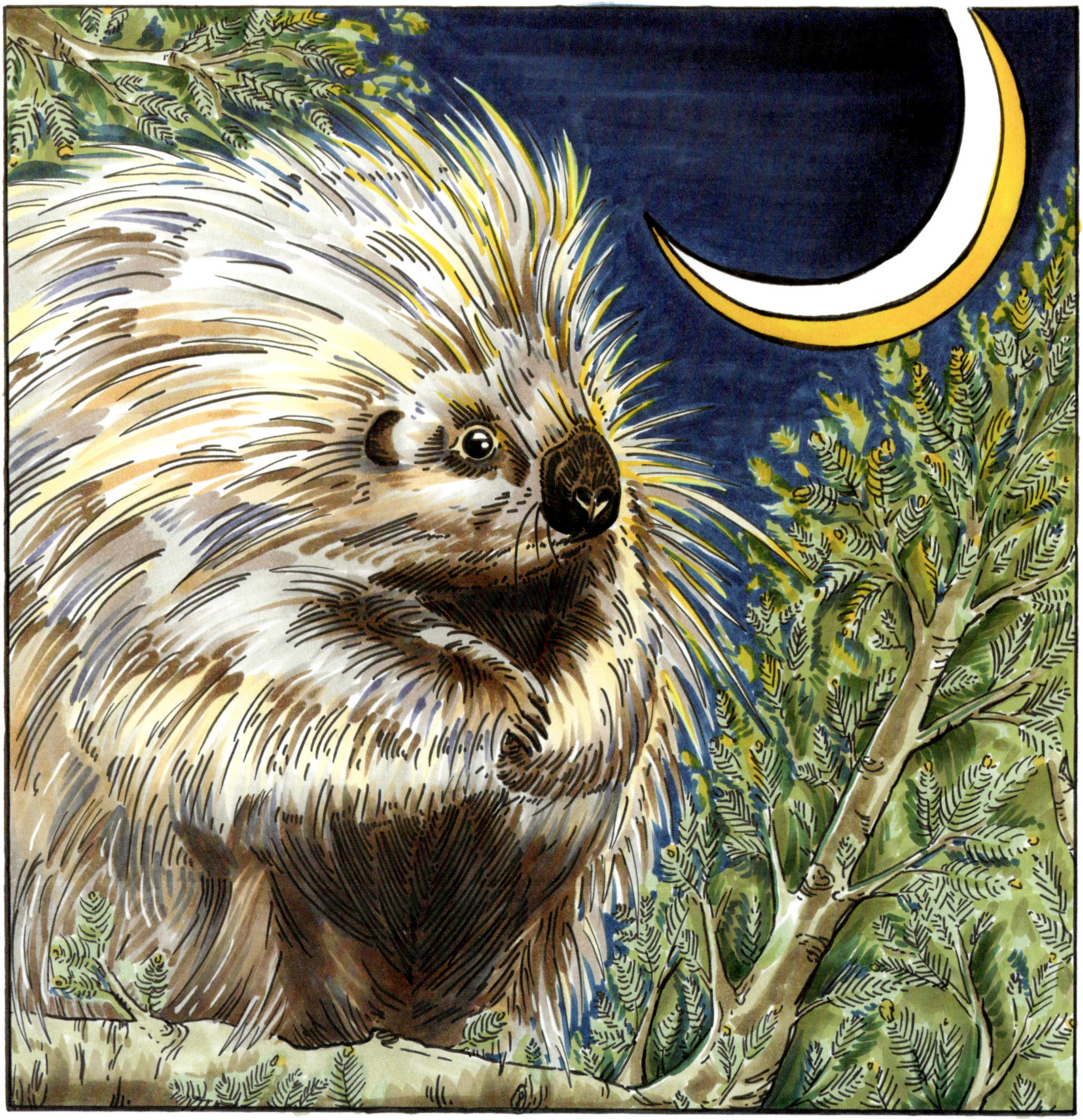

Prickly Porcupines

Porcupines are large, nocturnal herbivores that can be spotted traipsing about the mountainsides in Telluride and Mountain Village. A porcupine has approximately 30,000 quills on its body to provide protection from predators. Each quill is equipped with between 700 and 800 barbs nearest its tip, which is why they are so difficult to remove. Contrary to popular belief, these rodents can't actually shoot their quills, they are just easily shed and embedded into their unfortunate victim.

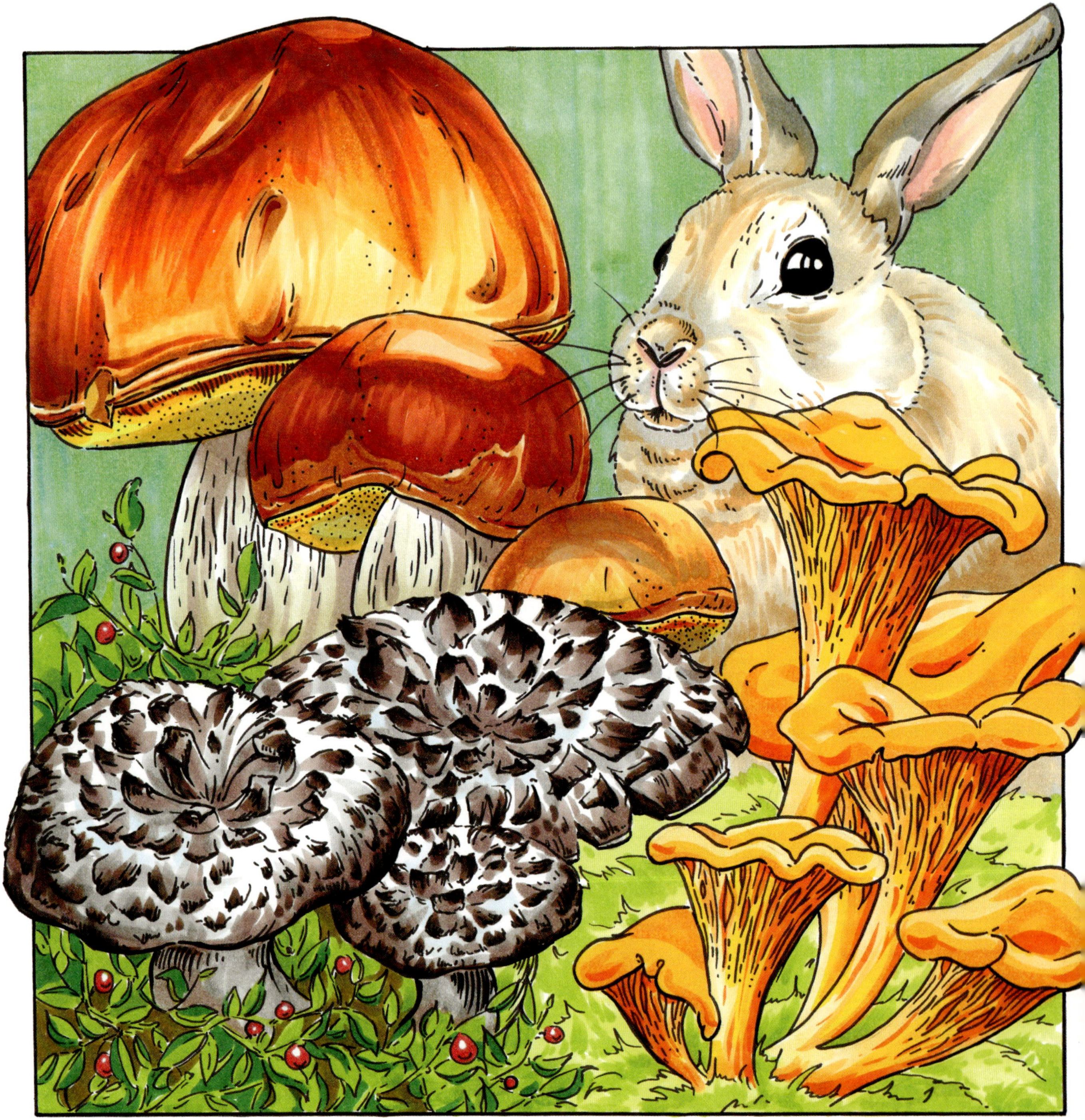

Quirky Quest

Fungi, such as boletes, chanterelles, hawk's wings and puffballs can be found hidden in the wilderness around Telluride. Foragers scour the forest's undergrowth for these earthy treasures, not only for a tasty snack, but also for their medicinal qualities. Seasoned mushroom hunters know to "trust, but verify" to ensure that the mushrooms are safe before they ingest them. You too can celebrate all things mycological at the Telluride Mushroom Festival in August, and make sure to catch the Main Street parade for a glimpse of some eccentric, mushroom themed costumes.

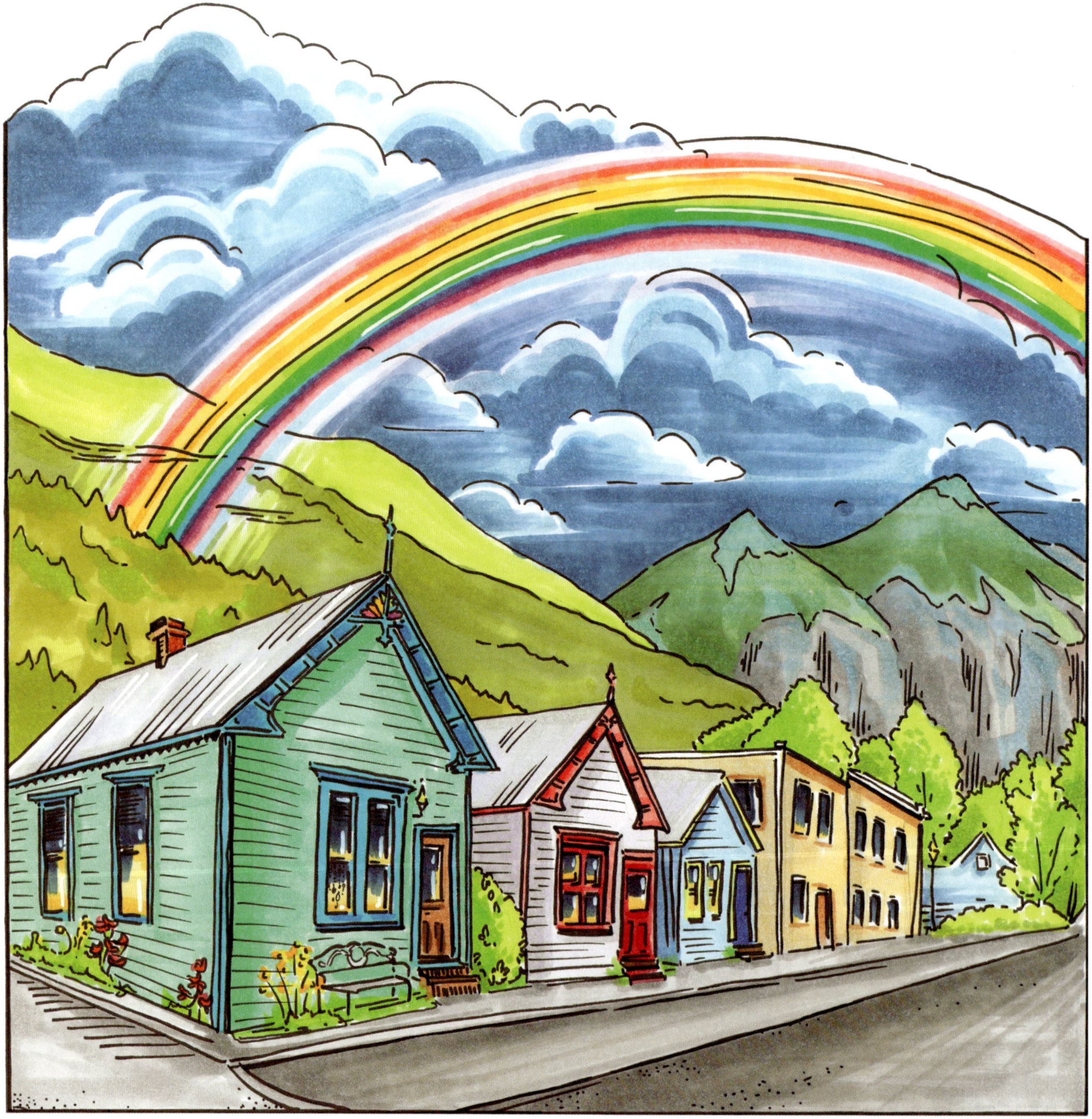

Radiant Rainbows

Rainbows normally occur when light is bent inside raindrops, but you can also spot them in mist, fog and dew. Double rainbows are formed when sunlight bounces inside the water droplet more than once before escaping, thus causing the colors in the bow to reverse. Isaac Newton added the colors orange and indigo to the spectrum in the mid-1600s, resulting in the mnemonic ROY G BIV. If you are in Telluride in the summer, you're sure to spot a vibrant arc or two spanning across the box canyon.

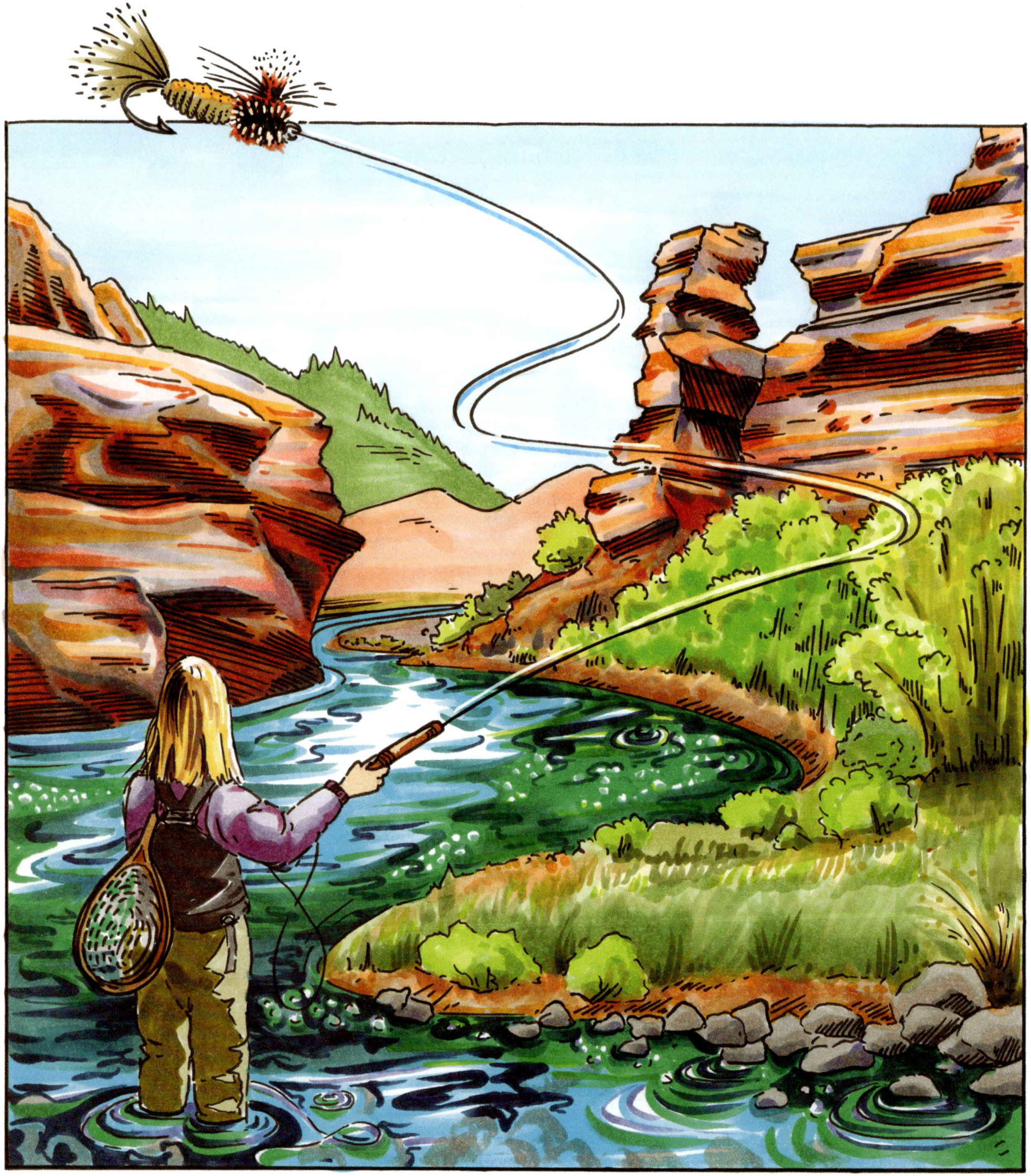

Snaking San Miguel

The San Miguel River begins in the San Juan Mountains above Telluride and stretches nearly 80 miles to join the Dolores River in the desert near Uravan. This pristine river draws in a number of fly fishing enthusiasts hoping to hook a fresh trout for dinner. Rafters, kayakers, tubers and people riding on SUPs take advantage of the increased water flow during the spring snowmelt. If you're walking along the River Trail in town, keep an eye out for evidence of beaver activity, such as gnawed tree stumps and beaver dams.

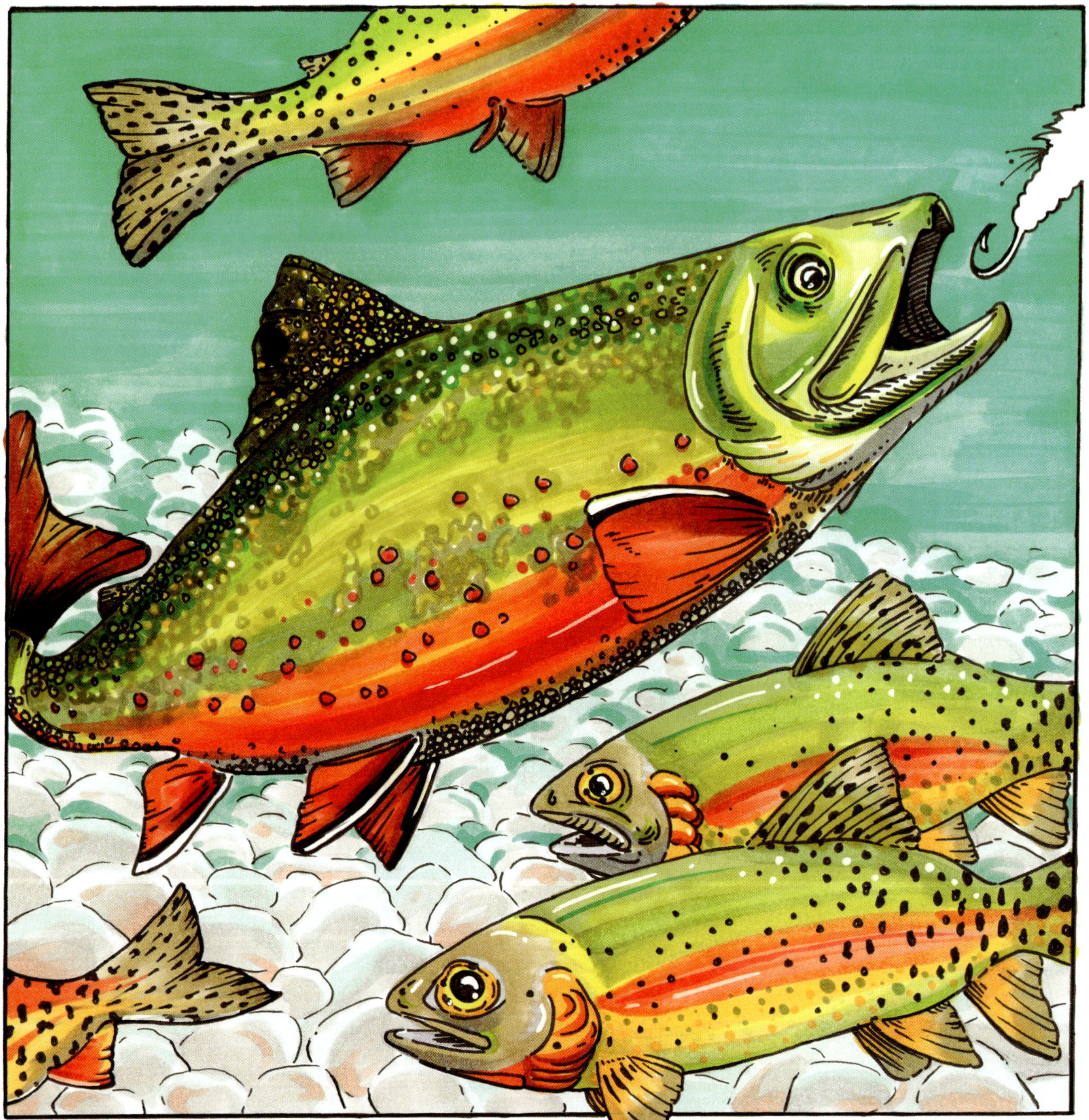

Teeming Trout

The rivers, ponds and lakes surrounding Telluride are all great places to spot a variety of trout, such as rainbow, brown, brook and cutthroat. Trout spend close to 90 percent of their time feeding on nymphs under the water's surface and are particularly fond of the stonefly. If you're interested in trying your hand at fly fishing, you can hire a local guide to get you geared up, teach you the proper techniques, and lead you to some hidden trout treasure troves. Even if you don't catch any fish, you are sure to take in some breathtaking scenery while you're out fishing!

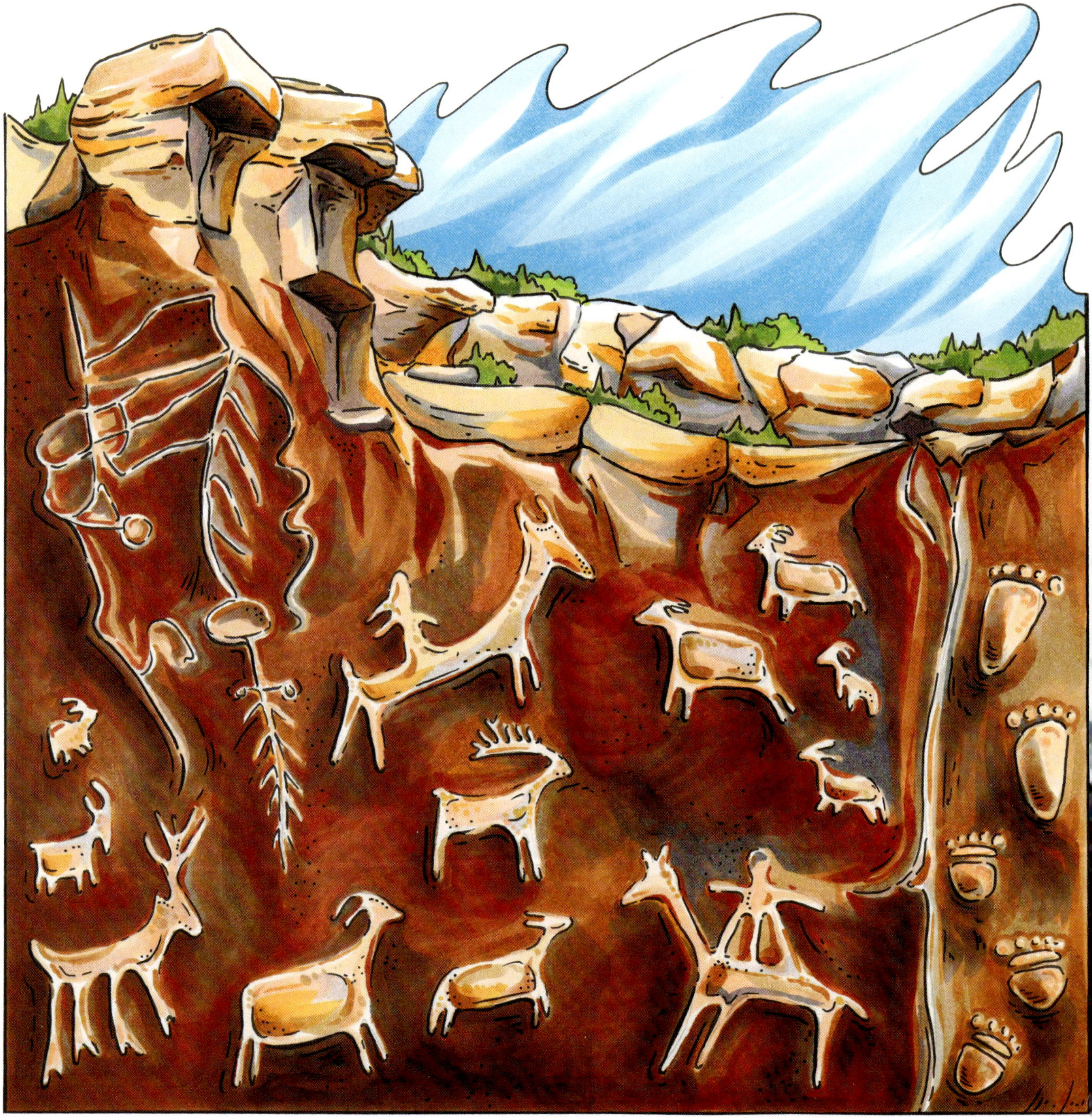

Uncompahgre Utes

For many centuries, the Uncompahgre Utes traveled to what is now Telluride in the summer, to set up camp and access the valley's plentiful hunting. By 1881, they were forcibly removed from their native homelands and were relocated to northeastern Utah. The Uncompahgre Ute Band was then made part of the larger Ute Tribe on the Uintah and Ouray Indian Reservation, where many of their descendents still reside today. You can learn more about Ute history and traditions through their oral storytelling and petroglyphs, or by visiting the Ute Indian Museum in Montrose, Colorado.

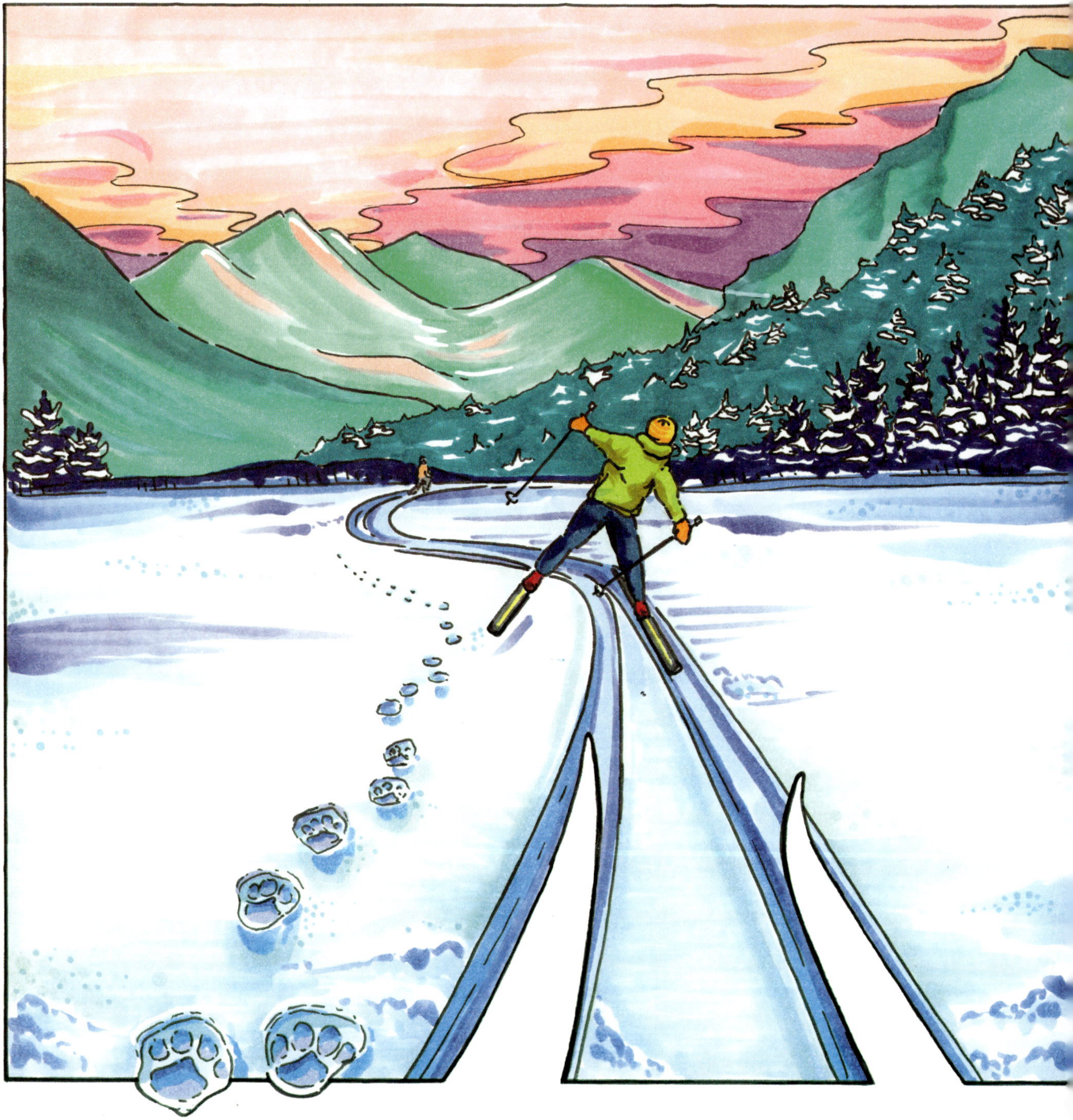

Vast Valley Floor

On May 9, 2007, a group of activists helped to secure the future of this precious open space just outside the town of Telluride. They ensured that it will forever remain a place that people can enjoy activities such as cross country skiing, mountain biking and hiking. It also allowed for the continued conservation of native animals' natural habitats and the restoration of the San Miguel River Basin. Although dogs are not allowed on the Valley Floor, you may be able to spot other animal tracks in the mud or snow such as elk, coyote or the elusive lynx.

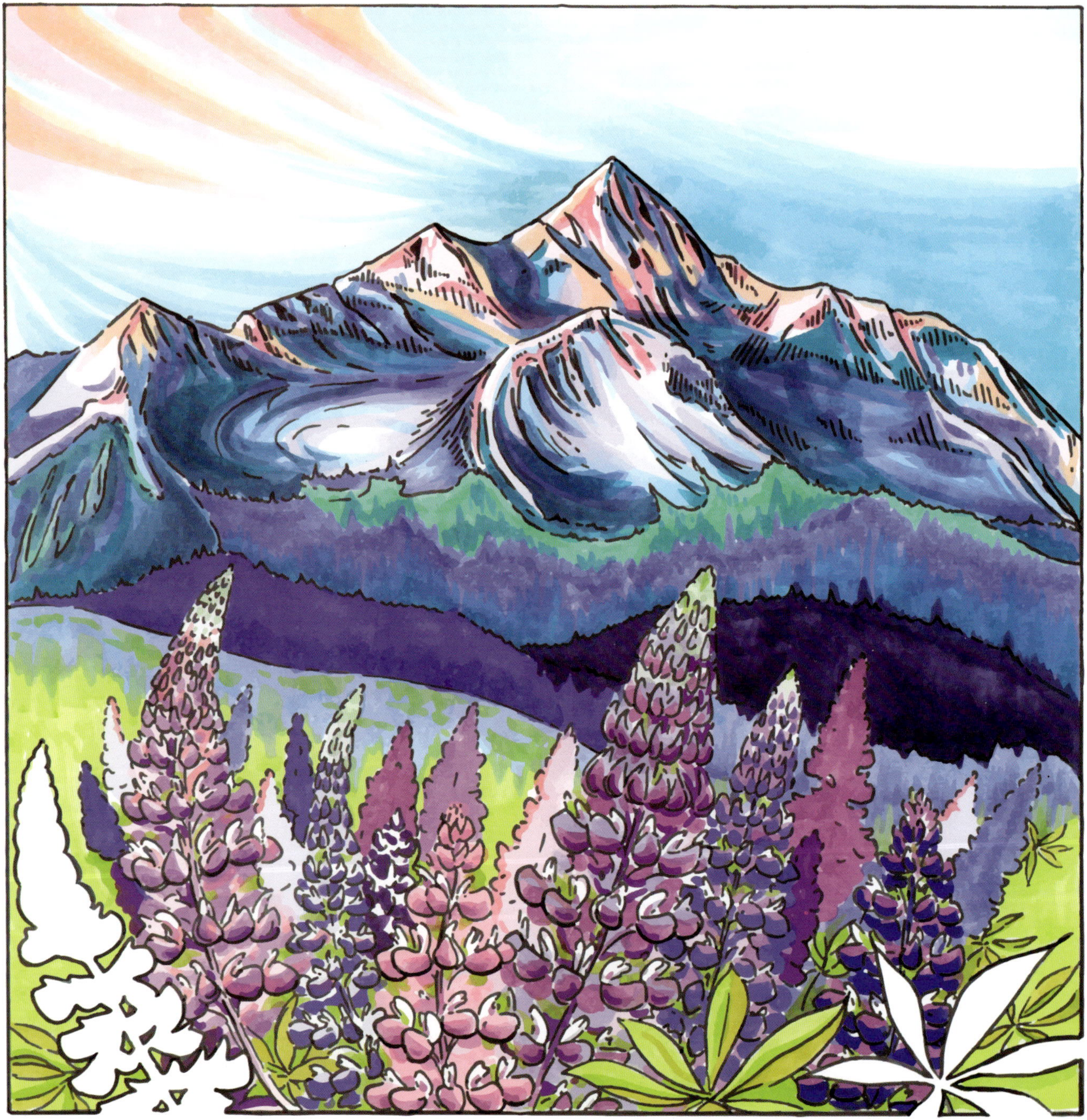

Whimsical Wilsons

Named after A.D. Wilson, a topographer of the 1870s who mapped out much of Colorado's Western Slope, Wilson Peak stands at a jarring 14,023 feet. Not to be confused with Mount Wilson, about two miles away, which measures in at a slightly taller 14,252 feet. The Wilsons are two of more than 50 Fourteeners that can be found in Colorado. You might even recognize Wilson Peak as the mountain that adorns Coors cans and bottles, even though the Coors Brewing Company is located about six hours away in Golden, Colorado.

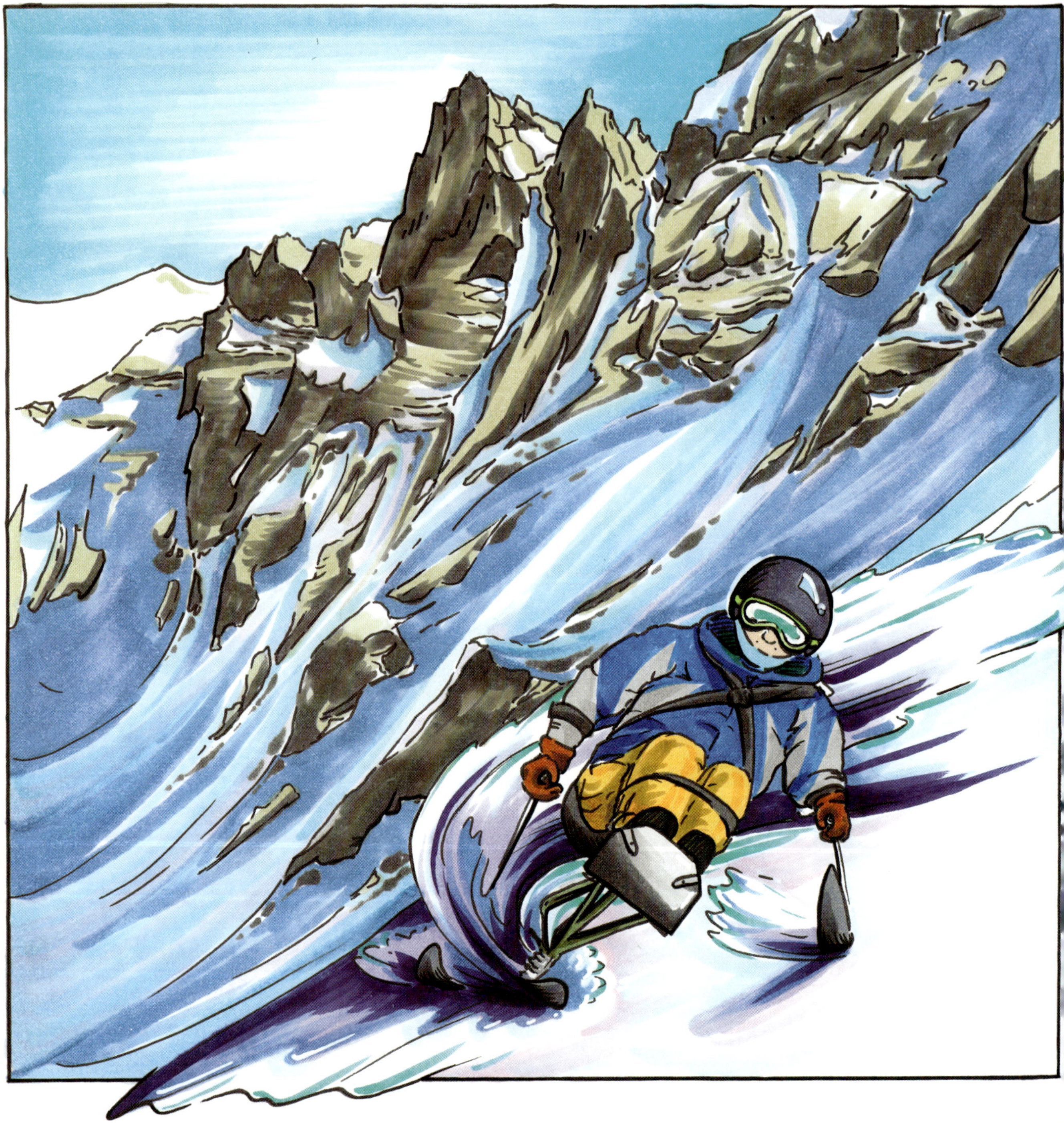

eXpert eXtremes

Bill "Senior" Mahoney was instrumental in transitioning Telluride from a mining town into a destination ski resort. After Joe Zoline moved to town in 1968, the two teamed up to create something bigger than the primitive tow rope in Town Park. In 1972, the Telluride Ski Area officially opened with five lifts and a day lodge. It has grown exponentially over the years into the resort that outdoor enthusiasts of all ages and skill levels know and cherish today. You can enroll in ski school or hire a personal instructor if you're looking to sharpen your skills to shred the gnar.

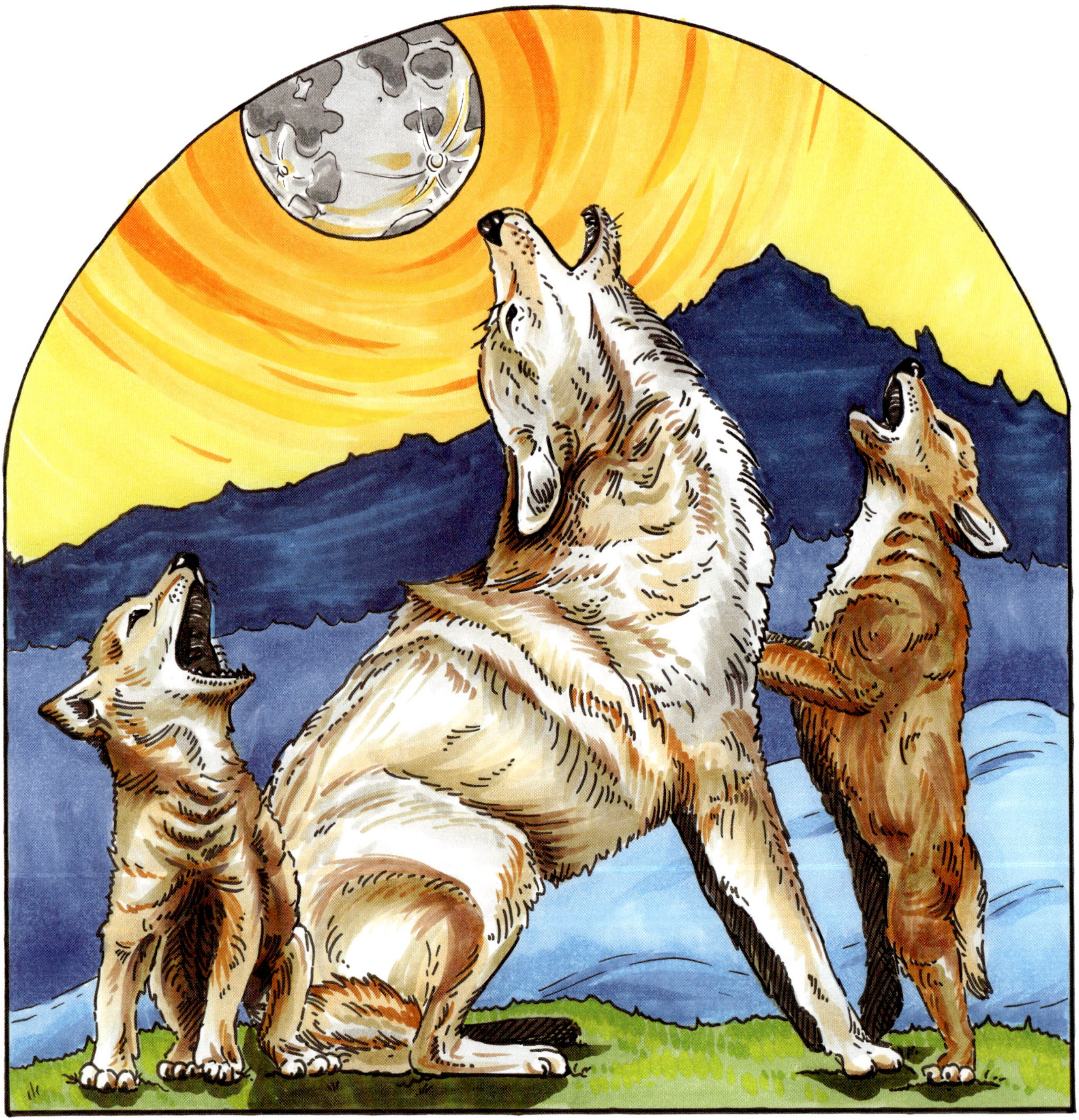

Yippy Yappers

Coyotes are intelligent, playful canids also know as "song dogs." When people hear coyote howls or yips, they often assume that they are hearing a large pack of animals. However, this is actually an auditory illusion called the *beau geste effect*, which can make two of these tricksters sound like seven or eight animals. Listen closely at dusk to hear their calls echo off the mountains around Telluride. Although their preferred menu consists of field mice and other small animals, make sure to keep your pets close by to be on the safe side.

Eider Creek
Mill Cree
Sneffels Highline
Deep Creek
Butcher Creek
Cornet Creek
Jud Wiebe
Floor Trail

Zigging Zags

One of the most popular summer activities in Telluride is hiking. You can hike to spectacular waterfalls, through fields of wildflowers, and up to high alpine lakes. With over 90 regional hiking trails of varying levels, you can be sure to find solace in nature. Some local favorites, by level of difficulty, are the Telluride River Trail, Bear Creek Falls and the Jud Weibe Trail. Be sure to pack plenty of water, snacks and layers because storms in the high country can be unpredictable and hiking at this altitude is no easy feat.